FIONA EVANS

Fiona studied Creative Arts (Drama) at Northumbria University where she first started writing. She spent many years working within community, youth and education settings, running drama sessions and writing plays in collaboration with different groups.

In 2004, Fiona wrote her first play *We Love You, Arthur* which was produced by New Writing North (NWN). It toured regionally and played the Assembly Rooms, Edinburgh, in 2005, receiving excellent reviews. In 2007, Fiona returned to the Assembly Rooms with *Scarborough* (originally produced by NWN in Newcastle as part of the Emerge/Bitesize scheme), which won a Fringe First Award, became the hottest ticket on the fringe, and transferred to the Royal Court Theatre, London, in 2008. Fiona's next play, the critically acclaimed *Geoff Dead: Disco for Sale* (commissioned by NWN, produced by Live Theatre and NWN, 2008) was about the mystery surrounding the deaths at the Deepcut Army Barracks. Chris Monks, Artistic Director of the Stephen Joseph Theatre in Scarborough, came to see it and was so impressed he commissioned Fiona to write a new play for the theatre: *The Price of Everything*. Other plays for theatre include *The Virgin of Stratford* (performed reading, Stratford East Theatre Royal, 2005).

As well as her theatre work, Fiona has written for radio, including *Beware the Kids* (co-written with Karen Laws), commissioned and directed by Kate Rowland for BBC Radio 3's Free Thinking Festival, 2009.

Fiona is a graduate of the BBC Writers Academy 2007, and has written for *Casualty*, *Doctors*, *EastEnders* and *Holby City*.

Other Titles in this Series

Fiona Evans

THE PRICE OF EVERYTHING

NICK HERN BOOKS

London

www.nickhernbooks.co.uk

A Nick Hern Book

The Price of Everything first published in Great Britain in 2010 as a paperback original by Nick Hern Books Limited, 14 Larden Road, London W3 7ST

Cover original artwork: Anonymous Design
Cover photo image: Tony Bartholomew Photography
Cover design: Ned Hoste, 2H

Typeset by Nick Hern Books, London
Printed in the UK by CLE Print Ltd, St Ives, Cambs, PE27 3LE

A CIP catalogue record for this book is available from the British Library

ISBN   978 1 84842 149 3

FSC
The mark of responsible forestry
TT-COC-003115
FSC Trademark © 1996 Forest Stewardship Council A.C

The Price of Everything was first performed at the Stephen Joseph Theatre, Scarborough, on 2 November 2010 (previews from 28 October), with the following cast:

EDDIE CARVER	Andrew Dunn
PAM CARVER	Julie Riley
RUBY CARVER	Jodie Comer

Director	Noreen Kershaw
Designer	Tim Meacock
Lighting Designer	Jim Simmons
Film and Editing	Martin Belderson

Filmed sequences in the original production featured the Stephen Joseph Theatre OutReach Community Actors: Lee Atkinson, Melissa Bar, Jayne Coyne, John Deans, Nadia Emam, Jennifer Garvey, Barbara Halsey, George Holden, Damon Hotchin, Mark Palmer, Vee Shrimpton, Sharon Stone, Bradley Thompson, Lee Ure, Michelle Wakefield, Dan Welch, Julia West, Ian Whitfield, Sharon Wooley and Patrick Young.

The production was supported by the Friends of the Stephen Joseph Theatre, Scarborough.

For Our Kath & Ray

A treasured sister and priceless friend.
My lovely brother-in-law and unofficial banker.

CECIL GRAHAM. What is a cynic?

LORD DARLINGTON. A man who knows the price
of everything and the value of nothing.

Lady Windermere's Fan, Oscar Wilde

Characters

EDDIE CARVER, *late forties. Flash barrow boy turned
    millionaire entrepreneur*
PAM CARVER, *mid to late forties. Well-preserved ex-beauty
    queen*
RUBY CARVER, *fifteen years old. Smart, confident teenager*

Setting

The play is set in a Cheshire manor house in Autumn 2010.

Note

Dialogue in [square brackets] indicates intention, not to be
spoken.

Text in *italic bold type* indicates audio and film instructions.

Dialogue in **bold type** indicates recorded speech, either as audio
or onscreen.

(In the original production, filmed sequences were screened on
four CCTV monitors placed within view of the audience, and
also on the TV screen which formed part of the set. During the
course of the play, random CCTV footage from outside the
manor played on the monitors. The sound of CCTV cameras
swivelling was used at appropriate points to help build tension
and cover scene changes.)

The characters and events depicted in this play are fictitious.
Any similarity to actual persons, living or dead, is purely
coincidental.

This text went to press before the end of rehearsals and so may
differ slightly from the play as performed.

ACT ONE

Scene One

The lounge in the Carvers' manor is an ostentatious place, a mishmash of old and new. EDDIE*'s shotgun has been left carelessly lying around – not in a prominent position. A huge arrangement of flowers sits in pride of place. Somewhere in the room will be* RUBY*'s book –* Complete Poems and Songs of Robert Burns *– and a dog's squeaky toy. The TV is a huge, top-of-the-range multimedia system.*

On the TV and CCTV monitors plays a recording of Eddie delivering a motivational business speech.

Simultaneously – EDDIE *appears at the top of the stairs with the remote control pointed at the TV, carrying a game of Monopoly. He is enjoying his performance and joins in, taking over. At some stage* EDDIE *will hide* RUBY*'s book out of sight.*

EDDIE. Business is about taking risks. Calculated risks. Before you make any big decisions you need to think things through. Understand your business. Suss out the opposition. Master the market. Before you invest… eat, drink, sleep and shite that business. You should know it better than you know your wife and kids.

Me? I like to plan. Always think things through. If I know what to expect, there'll be no surprises. It's all about retaining control. Have a strategy. Limit your losses. That doesn't mean being risk-averse. Like I've said… business is about taking risks. If you're not prepared to put your neck on the line, you shouldn't be in the game.

People often ask: 'Eddie, why did you decide to go into business? Why become your own boss?' The answer's easy: I'm unemployable. An awkward bastard with one hell of an ego. Who would be stupid enough to take me on? Only a madman… or my wife.

Polite laughter.

'But where do you get your drive to be an entrepreneur? What makes you succeed when so many have failed?' (*Pause for effect.*) I love making money... it makes me hard. There, I've said it. I play the market, drive a hard bargain, keep my eye on the bottom line and seal that deal. It's sexy.

Success depends on two things: on being able to recognise when your time has come, and on grabbing that moment by the balls and giving it a good old squeeze. To achieve your targets, you must adapt to change. Yes, have a strategy. But things don't always go according to plan. A good businessman will adjust to a situation, seize opportunities, maybe go with the flow, and then, when the time is right, take the plunge. Leap and the net will appear.

Loud clapping... as Eddie drinks in the applause, then exits.

Music over CCTV footage of the exterior of the house.

Scene Two

PAM *and* RUBY *enter the lounge, laden with shopping bags from exclusive boutiques.* PAM *has had a few drinks, she is tiddly but not drunk. The scene is good-humoured.*

PAM. Oh, straighten your face.

RUBY. It's a complete waste of money.

PAM. He got carried away.

RUBY. Showing off.

PAM. He did it for me.

> EDDIE *walks in with a huge, signed, soft-focus portrait of Kerry Katona – her massive cleavage on show.*

EDDIE. You should have seen Trevor's face when the hammer came down.

RUBY. Did it for you? I don't think so.

EDDIE. I did.

RUBY. Didn't.

EDDIE. Did.

RUBY. Didn't.

EDDIE. Didn't.

RUBY. Did.

EDDIE. Arh, got you.

RUBY. Not fair.

EDDIE (*to* PAM). I wanted your first auction to be a success.

PAM. I'll be patron of that charity before you know it. Queen of the Heart Foundation.

RUBY. You don't give to receive.

EDDIE. Who taught you that?

PAM *finds this amusing*.

RUBY. Nine thousand pounds! It's obscene.

EDDIE. I think it's a lovely photo.

RUBY. I meant your behaviour.

PAM. Darling, Daddy doesn't suit a hair shirt.

RUBY. We are in the middle of a recession. There were probably people in that room on the verge of losing their homes and Daddy's giving it largesse with Kerry Katona.

PAM. It's not our fault if the world economy is going belly-up, is it, Eddie?

EDDIE. It certainly isn't. Anyway, it's for your bedroom.

RUBY. You have got to be joking.

EDDIE. You used to like that band she was in.

RUBY. I liked one song when I was seven.

EDDIE (*admiring Kerry Katona's assets*). We could always put it up over the mantlepiece.

PAM. Keep the dog off the fire.

RUBY. Then I'd never be able to invite my friends round. (*Beat.*) Actually, where is he?

PAM. If that dog's asleep on my bed [I'll swing for him]…

RUBY. Goldy!

EDDIE. Who wants some champagne?

RUBY *spots her book in its hiding place.*

RUBY. What's that doing there?

EDDIE. Not tonight, put it away.

RUBY (*suspicious*). Did you hide it?

EDDIE. No. Come on, who's for champagne?

RUBY. What are we celebrating now?

EDDIE. The end of a wonderful day.

PAM. The start of my new career. Queen of Hearts. Anyway, we don't need an excuse – charity begins at home.

PAM *goes to exit.*

EDDIE. What are you doing?

PAM. I'll get it.

EDDIE. The champagne is usually my department.

PAM. Well, I fancy a change.

RUBY. Oooh… Mummy's being assertive.

EDDIE. I'll do it.

PAM. You've done quite enough today, you put your feet up and I'll see to the champagne.

PAM *exits and* EDDIE *concedes, turning his attention to* RUBY. *He opens his arms and she goes to him – they hug, this is obviously a regular thing.*

RUBY. Thanks, Daddy, I've had a fabulous day.

EDDIE. It's been fun, hasn't it?

RUBY. You didn't have to buy me all these clothes.

EDDIE. I thought you wanted them?

RUBY. Well, yeah. I'm not going to say no, am I? It isn't every day that I'm set free in Vivienne Westwood.

EDDIE. As long as you don't start wearing a safety pin through your nose.

RUBY *doesn't get the reference.*

RUBY. What?

EDDIE. Never mind. You'll look a million dollars.

RUBY. Everyone at school will be so jealous.

He sniffs her hair.

EDDIE. Have you been smoking?

RUBY. No.

EDDIE. Ruby. You know how I feel about smoking.

RUBY *takes out her phone and starts texting.*

RUBY. Hypocrite.

EDDIE. Oi!

RUBY. You used to.

EDDIE. *Used* to.

RUBY. I haven't been smoking.

EDDIE. I can smell it on you.

RUBY. I was standing outside with someone who was.

EDDIE. Who?

RUBY. Don't get all 'Victorian Dad' on me. I am allowed to talk to boys.

EDDIE. As long as that's all you're doing.

RUBY. Daddy!

EDDIE. I know what teenage boys are like.

RUBY. You should trust me.

EDDIE. I do. It's those little bastards I don't trust.

RUBY. I can handle spotty scholarship boys with wandering hands.

EDDIE. I don't like you talking like that.

EDDIE *takes the phone and puts it on a table, away from her.*

RUBY (*annoyed*). I'm nearly sixteen.

EDDIE. You're still my little girl.

RUBY. I won't be your little girl for ever.

PAM *enters with the champagne.*

PAM. Here we go… Hey, Rubes, did Tamsin see your jacket?

RUBY. I didn't have time to show her. (*Jangles her bracelet.*) But she loved my new Pandora Charms.

EDDIE. All the evils of the world wrapped around one pretty little wrist.

PAM. Eddie!

RUBY. I'll text her a picture of the jacket.

EDDIE. Not now.

PAM (*slightly mocking*). Dad's right. Family evening.

EDDIE *examines the champagne.*

EDDIE. You should have chosen a better vintage. Give it here, I'll change it.

PAM *retrieves the champagne from him.*

PAM. Ah-ah-ah… my turn to choose.

EDDIE. We should be having the best.

PAM. Relax. We've plenty of time.

EDDIE. Okay, have it your way.

PAM *opens the champagne, pours it into glasses as…*

RUBY. We don't have to cram everything into one night. We're not Kerry Katona.

PAM. Arh… leave Kerry alone.

EDDIE. I'd like to propose a toast. (*Pause.*) To my wonderful family.

PAM *and* RUBY (*giggling at his sentiment*). To us.

They all drink.

EDDIE. Right, everybody changed.

PAM. What?

EDDIE. Let's get our glad rags on.

RUBY. What for?

EDDIE. Do the Carvers need an excuse to have fun?

RUBY. When you put it like that…

PAM. I was saving mine for Ascot.

RUBY. I'm putting mine on.

RUBY grabs her bags and goes upstairs.

EDDIE. 'Ascot'?

PAM. Royal Ascot, actually.

EDDIE. When was this decided?

PAM. It's Ladies' Day. Viv asked… I could hardly say no.

EDDIE. Hardly.

RUBY (*from the stairs, a parting shot*). It's not Mum with the gambling problem.

EDDIE (*to PAM*). How does she know?

PAM. She's a very bright girl.

EDDIE. She's your daughter, not your best friend. You shouldn't offload onto her.

PAM. I didn't. Kids pick up on things.

EDDIE *seems to dwell on this – uneasy.* PAM *tries to win him round, playful…*

Now don't you start sulking, big boy, not on our special weekend. (*Beat.*) If you cheer up, I might even put on the red dress…

EDDIE. Now?

PAM. Right here, right now, if that's what you want?

EDDIE. Oh yes.

EDDIE *bangs on the music. Human League's 'Don't You Want Me Baby?'* PAM *recognises the track and starts singing along.*

I've done a playlist, all our favourites.

PAM. I don't know what's got into you lately, Eddie Carver, but I love it.

They dance around, singing, stripping and getting ready. Really having fun. EDDIE *grabs her and they start to kiss,* PAM *can feel his hard-on.*

Twice in one day, and I was beginning to think you'd gone off me.

EDDIE. Never.

They kiss more passionately, it threatens to go a bit far.

PAM. Ruby's upstairs.

EDDIE. Tease.

PAM. You always liked a challenge.

They fall onto the sofa… as they do, they lean on the remote which sets the DVD off –

It's a recording of their wedding day – all played through TV and CCTV monitors. It is bad quality and amateurish. Random pictures of guests arriving at or stood outside a modest country hotel, dressed in 1986 summer-wedding attire.

Jesus! What the… Eddie? What's this doing on?

EDDIE. I found it.

PAM. Where?

EDDIE. In one of those boxes in the barn.

PAM. What were you doing raking through them?

EDDIE. It was supposed to be a surprise. I got it transferred to DVD.

PAM (*touched*). Eddie. Look at the state of everyone.

Video cuts to inside the hotel. Guests congregating in the foyer at the foot of the stairs.

Oh my God, that's when they were waiting for us to come down... how embarrassing.

EDDIE. You weren't embarrassed at the time.

PAM. I'm sure my mother suspected.

EDDIE. She knew all right, gave me a right earbashing.

PAM. You never said.

EDDIE. Didn't want to spoil your big day.

PAM. It was your big day too. (*Beat.*) You're good at keeping secrets, aren't you?

EDDIE *doesn't respond, fixed on the TV –*

An embarrassed Eddie and Pam come downstairs to the waiting crowd, various cheers, jeers and catcalls.

Viv said she saw you going into the doctor's.

EDDIE. I bet you could still fit into that dress.

PAM. Eddie?

PAM *grabs the remote from* EDDIE *and pauses the video –*

On a two-shot of Pam and Eddie.

Viv saw...

EDDIE (*cuts in*). Not me.

PAM. She said it was definitely you.

EDDIE. She must have been mistaken.

PAM. That's what I told her. 'I would have known if Eddie had been to the doctor's. Eddie hates the doctor's. He'd have to be dying before he'd go to see a doctor.'

EDDIE. I must have a doppelgänger. There must be another handsome bastard in Cheshire.

PAM. She saw your car.

EDDIE. There are loads of Aston Martins in Alderley Edge.

PAM. Not with your private plate.

EDDIE. You don't believe me…?

PAM. It's not that, it's just…

EDDIE. Are you deliberately trying to ruin our night?

PAM. Not deliberately… I'm just worried about you…

EDDIE. Well, there's no need.

PAM. Are you sure…? (*Pause, tentative.*) It's just all this…

EDDIE. All what?

PAM. You making an effort…

EDDIE. I thought this is what you wanted?

PAM. It is… it's just…

EDDIE. Just what?

PAM. A bit too much.

EDDIE. Great.

PAM. Don't get me wrong… it's lovely… but it's not really you. The wedding video… taking the weekend off work… leaving your phone switched off, you've never done that… ever.

EDDIE. I want to spend time with my family, is that so bad?

PAM. No…

EDDIE. Well, can we just drop it, Pam, and have a nice time? Drink?

PAM declines. He pours them both a drink.

PAM. I said no.

EDDIE. Have a drink.

PAM. I don't want a sodding drink.

   RUBY *comes downstairs. Not ready.*

EDDIE. I thought you were getting changed?

RUBY. I can't find Goldy.

EDDIE. He'll be outside. Go on, get ready.

RUBY. How would he have got out?

EDDIE. You know what dogs are like.

PAM. He's a Labrador… not Houdini.

RUBY. When did you last see him?

EDDIE. This morning.

PAM. Was he in when you left to meet us?

EDDIE. Yes. No… I don't know.

RUBY. You didn't check?

EDDIE. I had a lot on my mind.

PAM. Like what?

   RUBY *goes to the door.*

EDDIE. Where are you going?

RUBY. To look for him.

EDDIE. Stay here. I'll go.

PAM. He is her dog.

EDDIE. I don't want her wandering about outside.

PAM. Why not?

EDDIE. Anything could happen.

PAM. For God's sake.

RUBY. Like what?

EDDIE. Anything.

PAM. It's like Fort Knox out there.

RUBY. I need to feed the ponies.

EDDIE. I'll do it.

PAM. You?

EDDIE. I've done it before.

RUBY. I'm coming with you.

EDDIE (*sharply*). No.

RUBY. Daddy!

EDDIE. My house, my rules. You set up the Monopoly.

RUBY. Monopoly?

EDDIE. You like Monopoly.

RUBY. I don't want to play stupid Monopoly.

PAM. Just do it, Ruby.

> EDDIE *exits*.

RUBY. You always take his side.

PAM. No I don't.

RUBY. It's pathetic.

PAM. Don't spoil things.

> PAM *picks up a copy of* Cheshire Life *and starts to flick through*.

RUBY. Me? I'm not the one who's acting all weird. (*Re: wedding image on TV, disapproving*.) Urrh, who put that on?

PAM. He just wants us to have a nice night.

RUBY. By keeping us under house arrest?

PAM. Stop being such a drama queen.

RUBY. I always feed the ponies. They like their routine.

PAM. I know, but...

RUBY. But what…?

PAM *decides not to say what's really on her mind.*

PAM. He's really making an effort.

RUBY. It may have escaped your notice, but the dog's missing.

PAM. And your father's gone to look for him. He's probably out chasing rabbits.

RUBY. Since when was Goldy interested in rabbits?

PAM. There's probably a bitch on heat at the farm.

RUBY. That's miles away. He's not a shark.

PAM. Dirty dogs will go to extreme lengths to get their ends away.

RUBY. Gross.

PAM. He'll turn up. Let's not spoil our day. We've had a lovely time, haven't we?

RUBY. That's it, bury your head in the sand. Better still, *Cheshire Life*.

PAM. What do you mean?

RUBY. When did Daddy last buy you flowers?

PAM *ignores the question.*

Last make a grand guilty gesture? I know he's profligate at the best of times, but today…

PAM. Oh, 'profligate'… is that a new word?

RUBY. No.

PAM. I might get one of those Twitter accounts.

RUBY *finds this highly amusing.*

RUBY. They're for people with something to say.

PAM. I have got something to say.

RUBY. Like what?

PAM *struggles to find something to say.*

PAM. Loads of stuff.

RUBY. 'Tweet Tweet: Major emergency. Snapped nail. Off for a manicure.'

PAM. You should become a stand-up comedian.

RUBY. I might.

PAM. Viv's got a Twitter.

RUBY. Viv's got halitosis, you wouldn't want that.

PAM. It's not halitosis. It's the red wine and fags.

RUBY. It still smells like shit.

PAM. So does your attitude, young lady.

RUBY. Careful, Mummy, you nearly had an opinion. Maybe you should Tweet it.

PAM. Why do you always have to belittle me?

RUBY (*winding* PAM *up*).
    Wee, sleekit, cowrin, tim'rous beastie,
    O, what a panic's in thy breastie!
    Thou need na start awa sae hasty…

PAM (*cuts in*). Oh, shut up.

RUBY. You never tell him to shut up.

PAM. 'Him'!? Show some respect. Your father doesn't try to undermine me.

RUBY. He's forever contradicting you.

PAM. So? As long as I get what I want, that's the important thing. Let him think he's the boss. He probably does know more than me.

RUBY. He pretends to be more knowledgeable. It's all about confidence.

PAM. Well, you'd know all about that.

RUBY. And that's suddenly a bad thing?

PAM. Course not.

RUBY. Women's liberation did actually happen.

PAM. So you've read a few books and you think you know it all.

RUBY. I know more than you.

PAM. I was only a child in the sixties.

RUBY. Grow up, Mummy, take some responsibility.

PAM. Have you been speaking to India's mum again?

RUBY. She's very interesting.

PAM. Is she really?

RUBY. And so cool.

PAM. Yes, well, we could all let ourselves go and wear tie-dye. That doesn't prove a thing.

RUBY. You've got it so wrong. She's got her own style like… Kate Moss.

PAM. Because she goes bra-less?

RUBY. She doesn't need one.

PAM. That's because she's flat-chested.

RUBY. Did you know that she used to date a rock star?

PAM. And I'm Jackie Onassis.

RUBY. She did. That really old man from The Rolling Stones.

PAM. Well, that narrows it down.

RUBY. Mick Jagger… I've seen the photos. She looked great… free love and all that…

PAM. 'Free love'? It's just men's way of getting something for nothing.

RUBY. So they should pay for it?

PAM. One way or another, darling, we all pay for it.

RUBY. Great, so my mother's a prostitute.

PAM. Ruby!

RUBY. What does that make Daddy?

PAM. If he hears you talk like this…

RUBY. A client… He can't be a pimp because he doesn't like you working.

PAM. I do work.

RUBY. Organising charity lunches, not exactly Hillary Clinton.

PAM. Thank God. Have you seen her thighs?

RUBY. Why do you always judge women on their looks?

PAM. I don't.

RUBY. Yes you do.

PAM. Looks are important.

RUBY. I'm not going to rely on mine, to get me by in life.

PAM. What's that supposed to mean?

RUBY. Forget it.

PAM. You've got to work with your assets, Ruby. MENSA weren't exactly banging on my door. I haven't done too badly.

RUBY. You married a millionaire.

PAM. Nothing wrong with being shrewd. Anyway, he wasn't that rich when I first met him.

RUBY. Did you marry Daddy for money or love?

PAM. Both. Only a fool marries for one or the other.

EDDIE *enters*.

RUBY. Did you find him?

EDDIE. No.

RUBY. Well, where is he?

EDDIE (*not sure where to start*). I don't want you getting upset.

RUBY. Oh God. No…

PAM. What's happened?

EDDIE. Nothing…

RUBY. He's hurt, isn't he?

PAM. Not the electric fence.

RUBY. Has he been frazzled?

EDDIE. Calm down.

RUBY. Is he dead?

EDDIE. He's fine.

PAM. Then where the hell is he?

EDDIE. I've told a little white lie.

PAM. What?

RUBY. I told you something was going on.

EDDIE. It's nothing to worry about.

PAM. What do you mean, 'a little white lie'?

EDDIE. I took him to the kennels.

PAM *and* RUBY *are perplexed.*

RUBY. The kennels?

EDDIE. The receptionist in the doctor's, her family have opened some new ones.

RUBY. He hates kennels.

PAM. Which receptionist?

RUBY. Why does he need to be in kennels?

EDDIE. For God's sake, one at a time.

PAM. Which receptionist?

EDDIE. The blonde one.

PAM. How do you know her?

EDDIE. I don't…

RUBY. He should be here.

EDDIE. He'll be in the lap of luxury.

PAM. How did you know she had kennels?

EDDIE. Trevor told me…

PAM *and* RUBY *talk in unison:*

PAM. Trevor? I might have known it would have something to do with…

RUBY. Goldy doesn't need to be in kennels. He hates…

EDDIE (*shouts over them both*). We're going away.

   PAM *and* RUBY *are taken aback.*

PAM. On holiday?

EDDIE. I thought that would get your attention.

PAM. You've had this planned all along?

EDDIE. It was supposed to be a surprise.

RUBY. I can't go on holiday.

PAM. Course you can. Where are we going?

EDDIE. Where have I been promising to take you for years? Where did you want to go on honeymoon?

PAM. No!

EDDIE. Yes.

   PAM *screams with delight.*

RUBY. I've got my LAMDA exams next week.

PAM. We can rearrange.

RUBY. I've been rehearsing, I've learnt that Robert Burns poem.

EDDIE. I'll sort something.

RUBY. And what about my GCSEs?

PAM. We'll get you a private tutor.

EDDIE. I'll bribe the buggers if I have to.

RUBY. If it's all the same to you, I'd like to pass on my own merit.

PAM. Course you do, darling. I love you, Eddie Carver.

EDDIE. Are we happy now?

PAM. We certainly are. Why didn't you tell us earlier?

EDDIE. Well, it wouldn't have been a surprise then, would it?

RUBY (*playing bored*). Where are we going?

PAM. Heaven.

PAM runs upstairs, excited.

Recorded voices, over…

MAN. They were a very close-knit family.

WOMAN. Such a lovely girl, bright, beautiful…

GIRL. She was the same age as me.

MAN. We're all really shocked.

WOMAN. Stunned.

Scene Three

EDDIE *and* RUBY *are setting up the game of Monopoly.*

RUBY. I've got a new one upstairs.

EDDIE. The new one's rubbish…

RUBY. What's wrong with it?

EDDIE. Doesn't have money.

RUBY. It's got credit cards.

EDDIE. Exactly. (*Shouting up the stairs.*) Pam… hurry up, we want to get started.

RUBY. What's the problem with credit cards all of a sudden?

EDDIE. Takes all the fun out of it.

RUBY. Harder to cheat.

EDDIE. Probably easier. But what's the point in playing, if people can't see you're winning?

RUBY. You're so competitive.

EDDIE. Competition is healthy.

RUBY. You take it too far.

EDDIE. I do not!

RUBY. What about my sports day?

EDDIE. I won fair and square.

RUBY. They've had to ban the fathers' sack race because of you.

EDDIE. Have they?

RUBY. It's nothing to be proud of.

EDDIE. It's health and safety gone mad.

RUBY. Sian's still not speaking to me.

EDDIE. Accidents happen.

RUBY. You practically rugby-tackled him to the floor.

EDDIE. He was in my way.

RUBY. You broke his arm.

EDDIE. Rubbish.

RUBY. You're lucky he didn't sue.

    PAM *appears at the top of the stairs dressed in her old wedding dress. She strikes a pose.*

PAM. Da-dah.

RUBY. Oh my God!

PAM. You were right. I can still fit into it.

EDDIE (*beaming*). Come here.

    PAM *runs down the stairs and into his arms.* EDDIE *whisks her up and spins her round.*

PAM. I told you the personal-training fees were worth it.

RUBY. Please tell me you're not taking it on holiday.

EDDIE. You look bloody lovely. This is just perfect. Shame I can't fit into me suit.

PAM (*re: the Monopoly set*). Where did you get that? It's out the bloody Ark.

RUBY. Says Miss Havisham.

EDDIE. It's mine.

PAM. You've kept it all this time?

EDDIE. Pamela, darling, I've had this longer than I've had you.

RUBY. Mum isn't a chattel.

EDDIE. All right, Germaine Greer. She'll be burning her bloody bra next.

RUBY. Is she the only feminist you know?

EDDIE. I know plenty.

RUBY. Like who?

EDDIE. The Greenham Common lot.

RUBY. What's Greenham Common?

PAM. Not so clever now.

EDDIE. Bunch of unwashed, lentil-munching lesbians.

RUBY. You're such a Neanderthal.

EDDIE. Emmeline Pankhurst… she's a feminist.

RUBY. Strictly speaking she's a suffragette, but I'll make a concession. She probably was a feminist. Continue…

EDDIE (*struggling*). Germaine Greer.

RUBY. You've had her.

EDDIE. Not bloody likely, face like a moose.

PAM *and* EDDIE *find this hilarious.*

RUBY. Come on, name one more…

EDDIE. Jordan.

RUBY. Jordan!? She's not a feminist.

PAM. Slapper more like.

RUBY. Mum!

PAM. Well…

EDDIE. I don't think the 'sisterhood' would approve of language like that.

PAM. I tell it how it is.

RUBY. Oh really, so what about men who shag around?

EDDIE. Watch your language, you.

RUBY. Trevor bandies that word around plenty and you don't have a problem with him.

EDDIE. Yes, well, Trevor's not my daughter.

RUBY. TITS!

EDDIE. Oi!

PAM. Ruby.

RUBY. So it's all right for you to ogle them, but I can't use the word.

PAM. When have you been ogling tits?

EDDIE. I haven't been ogling tits.

RUBY. So you bought that picture because Kerry's got a nice smile?

EDDIE (*caught out, covers*). Yes. I like her… face. She's a bonny lass.

PAM. Pull the other one, it's got bells on.

EDDIE (*re: picture*). She is.

PAM. I don't mind you looking…

RUBY. So that isn't demeaning?

PAM. It's only a picture.

RUBY. That's where it all starts. Then they can't help themselves.

EDDIE. Rubbish.

RUBY. I caught you checking out Tamsin's tits at the auction.

EDDIE. I did not!

PAM. You better bloody not have, she's fifteen.

RUBY. She thought it was hilarious.

EDDIE. 'Hilarious'?

PAM. Eddie!

RUBY. He couldn't keep his eyes off them.

PAM. You could hardly miss them with that top she very nearly had on.

RUBY. So it's Tamsin's fault…

PAM. Takes after her mother.

RUBY. Viv's your best friend.

PAM. So?

RUBY. So it's Viv and Tamsin's fault that my father's a pervert?

EDDIE. I am not a pervert. Can we just drop the tit conversation…

RUBY. If we must, but you can't really think Jordan's a feminist.

EDDIE. Can we just get on with the game?

RUBY. Not until you answer my question.

PAM. It's your fault for setting her off.

RUBY. Come on, Dad, robust debate is essential for a healthy and democratic society.

EDDIE. I prefer a benign dictatorship.

PAM. Can I be First Lady?

RUBY. I'm waiting… how's Jordan a feminist?

EDDIE. She's got more balls than most blokes I know.

RUBY. Acting like a 'bloke' does not mean you're a feminist.

EDDIE. She's a successful businesswoman.

RUBY. Capitalist not feminist.

PAM. I'm getting bored.

EDDIE. Since when did she get so clever?

RUBY. Since you started paying for my education.

PAM. Since she started hanging around with India.

EDDIE. Who's India?

PAM. Her new best friend.

RUBY. Jealousy is unbecoming in a woman of your age.

PAM. Can we get on with the game, please?

EDDIE. Go on… pick, you can have whatever you like.

> PAM *and* RUBY *look to each other – 'Anything?' RUBY decides to test him.*

RUBY. Anything?

> EDDIE *nods.*

The racing car.

EDDIE. The racing car?

RUBY. You said I could choose…

EDDIE. You usually want the dog.

RUBY. I fancy a change.

EDDIE. Anything but the racing car…

PAM. Eddie!

EDDIE. I'm always the racing car.

RUBY. Well, isn't it about time someone else had a turn?

EDDIE. It's my lucky charm.

RUBY. I thought you didn't believe in 'all that nonsense'.

EDDIE. Lucky charms are different to fate. Fate is an excuse for losers to sit on their arse, fail and blame everyone else.

RUBY. A touch harsh, even by Stalin's standards.

PAM. Not everybody has your drive, Eddie.

EDDIE. Well, they should have.

PAM. I believe that certain things are meant to be.

RUBY (*teasing*). Like you and Dad?

PAM. Yes, actually. One way or another we all end up in the place we deserve.

RUBY. And that place is…?

PAM. Is here. Us living in this house. It's our destiny.

RUBY. What do you reckon, Dad? Is our fate written in the stars?

EDDIE. I'm just a businessman, Mills and Boon's your mother's department.

RUBY. Okay, were you destined to be a successful entrepreneur, or did you do it yourself?

EDDIE. I did it with lots of hard work and determination. That's the trouble with this world… too many lazy bastards…

PAM. Eddie!

EDDIE. It's true.

PAM. Language! No wonder she's got a potty mouth.

EDDIE. Lazy individuals who can't wait to have a pop at life's winners. They hate success. They're jealous…

RUBY. Envious.

EDDIE (*on a roll*). Bank managers, planning officers… the boring brigade, parasites and leeches… slowly sucking the life out of you.

RUBY. Wasn't Gramps a bank manager?

PAM. I think that's the only reason Daddy married me.

EDDIE. Rubbish! (*Beat.*) It was to spite your mother.

They all see the funny side.

PAM. Daddy never really saw eye to eye with Gramps.

EDDIE. They thought I was a mouthy barrow boy.

PAM. Flash Harry who would amount to nothing. But Daddy proved them wrong. Didn't you, love?

EDDIE *hands* PAM *the playing piece in the shape of an iron.*

EDDIE. Recognise one of them?

PAM. I'm not having the iron.

EDDIE. So you do remember what they look like.

PAM. That's what the cleaner's for. I'll have the battleship.

EDDIE. Why the battleship?

PAM. No reason.

EDDIE. There's always a reason.

Pause.

PAM. I used to go out with a sailor.

EDDIE. No you didn't.

PAM. I think I should know.

EDDIE. When?

RUBY. Mum did have a life before she met you.

PAM. He was an officer, actually, very handsome.

EDDIE *reluctantly hands over the battleship.*

My mum liked him.

RUBY *laughs.*

EDDIE. Have you picked your piece yet?

RUBY. The racing car.

EDDIE. Should we toss for it?

RUBY. No. I want the car.

EDDIE. I want never gets.

RUBY. That's not what you taught me.

EDDIE (*reluctantly concedes*). Go on then. I thought it would be against your green credentials.

RUBY *and* PAM *start giggling.*

RUBY. It is.

PAM. She's only winding you up.

EDDIE *cheers*.

RUBY. You can keep your gas-guzzling motor.

EDDIE. Don't start lecturing me about my carbon bloody footprint.

RUBY. The Cheshire Yeti. You make Jeremy Clarkson look positively evolved.

PAM. I love him.

EDDIE. Oh yeah?

RUBY. Permission to vomit.

PAM. Only because he reminds me so much of you. Do that thing he says. It's so funny.

EDDIE. 'A Range Rover, doing 10,000 miles a year, produces less pollution a day, than a cow farting.'

EDDIE *does a comedy fart in* RUBY*'s face*.

RUBY (*sarcastic*). How hilarious.

PAM. He's got a point, you know. I was listening to the radio the other day and it said pets were worse than fast cars and air travel.

EDDIE. Maybe we should lessen our carbon hoofprint and get rid of the ponies?

PAM. Don't tease her.

RUBY. Actually, I might have to get rid of them.

PAM. Don't be ridiculous. Why on earth would you have to do that?

RUBY. To go travelling.

EDDIE. 'Travelling'?

PAM. You aren't going travelling.

EDDIE. This is the first I've heard of it.

PAM. And it'll be the last. You're not going.

RUBY. Why not?

PAM. It's dangerous. Isn't it, Eddie?

RUBY. I'll be with India.

PAM. Like she'll be much use fighting off a six-foot axe-
wielding lunatic in the outback. What's she going to do, slap
him with her jewelled flip-flop?

RUBY. You're so blinkered.

PAM. Tell her, Eddie, she's not going.

EDDIE. You've never mentioned this before.

RUBY. You've never asked. We've been planning it for ages.

PAM. How are you going to afford it? Because we won't be
funding no trip.

RUBY. So you only pay for things that you want me to do?

PAM. Yes.

EDDIE. Should we just get on with the game?

PAM. You're not going.

RUBY. You can't stop me.

PAM. What's this big plan then?

RUBY. If necessary, we'll sell the ponies to pay for the trip.

PAM. 'Sell the ponies'?

EDDIE. She's winding you up, now.

RUBY. I'm being serious.

PAM. You'd sell your ponies?

EDDIE. Course she wouldn't.

RUBY. Will you stop telling me what I would and wouldn't do.

EDDIE. You love those ponies.

PAM. Ponies are worth next to nothing these days, you'll be hard
pushed to give them away. It'll cost you more than a few
grand to go travelling.

RUBY. Youth hostels are cheap.

EDDIE. You couldn't live without your ponies.

RUBY. Course I could.

PAM. She couldn't. Anyway, what about the equestrian business?

RUBY. What about it?

PAM. We've looked into sites and everything, haven't we, Eddie?

EDDIE. You don't want to go into business?

PAM. Course she does, it's her dream to set up an equestrian business.

RUBY. Well, I've changed my mind. I want to be a vet.

PAM. Since when?

EDDIE. You could have told us. Do you know the effort we've been to…

RUBY. Sorry, Daddy.

PAM. 'Sorry'? Your father has spent a fortune buying up land.

RUBY. Well, nobody asked me.

EDDIE. Just drop it, Pamela, it doesn't matter.

PAM. Yes it bloody does. (*To* RUBY.) You wanted this…

RUBY. No, Mum, you wanted it. I want to spread my wings… see the world…

PAM. Since when?

EDDIE. We're going on holiday, aren't we?

RUBY. No offence, but a five-star hotel on a gated complex is not exactly travelling.

PAM. Yeah well, 'travelling' is overrated.

EDDIE. Thank you, Judith Chalmers, very helpful.

PAM. Well…

RUBY. We want to experience the culture.

PAM. 'We'?

EDDIE. End up with bloody dysentery, more like.

RUBY. You're so racist.

EDDIE. What's racist about dysentery?

RUBY. You're casting aspersions on other cultures. When I travel I want to see the *real* country. Mix with the indigenous population.

PAM. India's put you up to this, like the vegetarianism and the carbon bloody offsetting.

RUBY. I do have my own opinions, unlike some.

PAM. What's that supposed to mean?

EDDIE. Can we just get on with the fucking game?

PAM. Sod the bloody game. I don't even like Monopoly.

EDDIE. Yes you do. You love it.

PAM. No, Eddie, you love it.

EDDIE. We played it the night of the storm, when the television went off. We had a great time, a real family night.

RUBY. That was years ago, Dad.

EDDIE. But we had a brilliant time.

PAM. You cheated.

EDDIE. I did not! I was the banker.

RUBY. And your point is…?

> RUBY *casually goes over to the window and looks through the curtains.*

PAM. You were squirrelling away money.

RUBY. And you said you landed on Mayfair and you'd only thrown six on the dice.

EDDIE. Come away from the window.

RUBY. I'm trying to admire the view.

PAM. You did cheat.

EDDIE. Mistakes happen.

RUBY. I can't wait for the light nights.

PAM. You robbed us blind.

EDDIE. So you don't want to play?

PAM. No...

> RUBY *reacts, she sees something at the window.*

RUBY. There's someone outside.

PAM. What?

RUBY. A man, over by the stables.

> EDDIE *goes for his shotgun.*

PAM. Call the police.

EDDIE. No.

> PAM *picks up the phone. Presses the buttons – it's not working.*

I said no.

PAM. The line's dead.

RUBY. Daddy, put the gun away.

PAM. What's happened to the phone?

EDDIE. You stay inside.

PAM (*to* RUBY). Use your mobile, call the police.

> EDDIE *loads his gun.*

RUBY. Daddy!

PAM. Eddie, don't go outside.

EDDIE. Stay here.

RUBY. Daddy, stop. You're scaring me.

EDDIE. Don't worry, sweetheart. I'll sort them out.

PAM. You'll get arrested.

EDDIE. This is my property.

PAM. It's not worth it.

RUBY. Daddy, put the gun away.

PAM. You can't go round shooting people.

PAM *blocks his way.*

Calm down, Eddie. (*To* RUBY.) Find your phone, call the
bloody police.

EDDIE. Get out of the way.

PAM. No.

RUBY. Stop it!

EDDIE. I'm warning you.

RUBY. I was only joking.

EDDIE *turns to face her, the gun is pointing at* RUBY.

EDDIE. What?

RUBY. I'm sorry.

EDDIE *is now shaking. He can't speak.*

I thought it would be a laugh.

PAM. You stupid… stupid girl.

RUBY. I'm sorry.

PAM. Are you all right, Eddie?

RUBY. Put the gun down, Daddy… please.

EDDIE *is on the verge of tears. He slowly uncocks the gun
and sinks to the floor, burying his head in his hands.*

Don't cry.

PAM. Look what you've done.

RUBY. It was supposed to be a joke.

PAM. A joke? Does this look like a fucking joke?

EDDIE *looks up and he's laughing. They all start laughing,
nervously.*

EDDIE. She was only joking. Those acting lessons are certainly
paying off.

Lights fade.

CCTV monitors flicker on –

***Eddie and Pam's wedding video. In church, mostly shot
from a distance, but you can make out Eddie and Pam
sitting at the altar as the priest gives his reading:***

PRIEST. **Not everyone who says to me, 'Lord, Lord,' will
enter the Kingdom of Heaven, but only he who does the
will of my Father who is in Heaven. Therefore everyone
who hears these words of mine and puts them into
practice is like a wise man who built his house on the rock.
The rain came down, the streams rose, and the winds blew
and beat against that house; yet it did not fall, because it
had its foundation on the rock. But everyone who hears
these words of mine and does not put them into practice is
like a foolish man who built his house on sand. The rain
came down, the streams rose, and the winds blew and beat
against that house, and it fell with a great crash.'**

The screens go blank.

Scene Four

EDDIE, PAM *and* RUBY *are playing Monopoly. The
atmosphere is awkward.*

EDDIE. I told you it would be fun.

PAM. You did.

EDDIE. You are having a good time?

In unison:

RUBY. Yeah, great.

PAM. Course we are.

EDDIE. Good. Your turn, Rubes.

RUBY *throws the dice, moves to Community Chest.*

PAM. Community Chest… could be good, could be bad.

EDDIE *picks up the card, reads:*

EDDIE. 'Congratulations, you have won second prize in a beauty contest. Collect ten pounds.'

RUBY. A beauty contest?

EDDIE. Nothing wrong with beauty contests.

PAM. Second? Never mind, Rubes.

EDDIE *hands her a Monopoly tenner.*

EDDIE. Ten pounds.

PAM. I could've been Miss Great Britain.

RUBY. Per-lease.

EDDIE. She could.

PAM. I was Miss North-West 1985.

RUBY. No you weren't.

PAM. Don't sound so surprised.

EDDIE. Your mother was the best-looking lass in South Manchester.

RUBY. Not much of an achievement, I'm guessing.

PAM. Cheeky madam. You didn't get your looks from your father's side of the family.

EDDIE. I was no slouch myself.

RUBY. Were you really a beauty queen?

PAM. Yes.

RUBY. How embarrassing.

PAM. Thanks.

RUBY. Where's the photos?

PAM. I haven't got any.

RUBY. You must have photos.

EDDIE (*lustful*). Linda Lusardi meets Kelly LeBrock in a white sprayed-on swimsuit.

RUBY. Gross.

PAM. It was the eighties. (*Beat*.) Anyway, I tore the photos up.

RUBY. No wonder.

PAM. That's right, I'm just a figure of fun, a big joke.

EDDIE. You are not.

PAM. I gave up my dreams of becoming Miss Great Britain for you two.

RUBY. Don't blame me, I wasn't even born.

EDDIE. I didn't make up the stupid rules.

RUBY. What rules?

EDDIE. A *Mrs* couldn't enter a beauty contest for *Miss* Great Britain.

   PAM *throws the dice*.

RUBY. You gave up your dreams for Dad?

EDDIE. I was quite a catch.

PAM. My mother didn't think so.

EDDIE. Double. Throw again.

RUBY. Do you ever regret it?

   Beat.

PAM. No.

EDDIE. You paused.

PAM. No I didn't.

   PAM *throws the dice*.

RUBY. You definitely paused.

   PAM *moves her piece. Not noticing it's on Park Lane.* EDDIE *quickly throws the dice*.

   Mum, you missed out on Park Lane.

PAM. Oh… why didn't you say?

RUBY. I can't play for you.

PAM. I was distracted.

EDDIE. All part of the game. Double bubble, me again.

RUBY. You do regret it, don't you?

PAM. Yes. (*Beat.*) But only when I'm losing at Monopoly.

EDDIE. Tactics. Be careful, she's ruthless.

PAM. Course I don't regret it... I've got a wonderful life, the best family in the whole world and... a wardrobe full of Jimmy Choos!

EDDIE *throws the dice. And cheers.*

EDDIE. Yes, what a beauty. One, two, three, four, five, six and lucky seven. Mayfair – buying.

The intercom goes. EDDIE *freezes.* RUBY *goes to answer it.*

Stay where you are.

PAM. Eddie!

EDDIE. I don't want anyone to answer it.

PAM. This is getting a bit bizarre.

RUBY. It'll be Tamsin.

EDDIE. Tamsin?

PAM *presses the remote –*

Tamsin appears on the TV and CCTV monitors.

RUBY. See, told you.

Intercom buzzes.

She's got my favourite bikini. If I'm going to Barbados, I need my pink bikini.

EDDIE. I'll buy you a new one.

RUBY. I want my old one.

PAM. It does look lovely on her.

RUBY. She won't be long, she's only dropping it off.

EDDIE. How's she got here?

Intercom buzzes.

PAM. Trevor or Viv will have given her a lift. Answer it.

EDDIE. No. They can't come in.

EDDIE *gets the remote and switches the CCTV off –*

Tamsin disappears.

RUBY. They know we're here.

PAM. For God's sake, Eddie.

The buzzer sounds continuously. EDDIE *goes over to intercom.*

RUBY. Hurrah. Finally.

He rips it off the wall.

Oh my God.

PAM. Eddie! What the hell?

EDDIE. It's a family night.

PAM. You're being ridiculous.

RUBY*'s phone starts ringing.*

RUBY. It's Tamsin.

PAM. Give it here.

EDDIE. They're not coming in.

PAM *answers before* EDDIE *can grab it.*

PAM (*on phone, putting on a good front*). Tamsin? Sorry, darling, Ruby's in the shower… Oh, the intercom's not working… Listen, you stay where you are and I'll come and collect it from the gate. Okay, my love, see you soon.

PAM *clicks off the phone.*

There, problem solved, you get your bikini and we don't get disturbed. For God's sake, Eddie, you're taking this family thing a bit too far. You're going to ruin the whole bloody night.

EDDIE. I'm sorry, you stay here, I'll go. I could do with the fresh air. I really am sorry, I'll make it up to you. I just want everything to be perfect.

EDDIE *exits*.

RUBY. He's nearly fifty and he still thinks perfect exists.

RUBY *goes to exit, putting on her wellies*.

PAM. Where are you going?

RUBY. To check on Jasper and Lou Lou.

PAM. Your father's done it.

RUBY. I haven't said goodnight to them.

PAM. Don't act as if you care. Five minutes ago you were waving them off to the knacker's yard.

RUBY. I'm selling them. I'll make sure they go to decent homes.

PAM. Once they've gone, you've no control over where they end up. Could even be the hunt, torn limb from limb by bloodhounds. Could even end up as glue.

RUBY. You're only saying that to put me off travelling.

PAM. I'm not going to sugar-coat this for you, Ruby.

RUBY. Just because you gave up your dreams, don't expect me to. Now excuse me while I say goodnight to my ponies.

RUBY *exits.* PAM *pours herself a large drink. She looks at the photo of Kerry Katona.*

PAM. Kerry... Kerry... Kerry... Where did it all go wrong?

Queen of the Jungle, and now look at you... not even the face of frozen-prawn vol-au-vents. You should have stuck with that good-looking one from Westlife. You did the hard bit. Not every woman could paint on a smile after their husband shagged a lap dancer on his stag night. You were a trooper... a true professional. You had a room full of celebrity guests and photo contracts worth thousands. One day it's *Hello! OK!* The next... a taxi-ride to oblivion. How the mighty have fallen...

Can you believe my daughter wants to be a vet? Where's the ambition in that? Not exactly glamorous. I've seen *All Creatures Great and Small*... no profession for a young lady. Anyway, I'm sure her arms aren't long enough... just as well... that procedure would ruin manicured acrylics.

It's not that I've anything against women having a career. I've got one... Ruby and Eddie... they're my career. You see, I've got the best of both worlds... and on occasions the worst. Because, I'm telling you, he's doing my head in. Tonight is not quality time as far as I'm concerned. Not that I'd let him know. Wouldn't want to rock his yacht. There's more than one actress in this house. I deserve an Oscar for some of my performances.

I prefer it when he's out at work. *He* prefers it when he's out at work. He hunts and I gather... designer shoes, mainly.

PAM *picks up* EDDIE'*s coat, admiring. She puts it on... relishing the feeling, the material, the smell... the wealth.*

People say it's what's inside you that counts. In my experience... it's who's inside you. And looks do matter. People judge you. All the time. You know that more than anyone. They might say they don't, but they do. I do it. It's human nature. They've done studies in America which prove attractive people get better treatment and service. Image is everything. Would I be with Eddie if he cleaned the streets or signed on? Course I bloody wouldn't. Not because I'm shallow... but because I fell in love with a winner – a man with pride in himself, with drive, dreams and ambition. And I know for certain that he wouldn't be with me if I let myself go. If I was a twenty-stone heifer with a face like a bag of spanners, no way... I wouldn't see his arse for dust. And you know what...? I wouldn't blame him. Because that's not part of the deal...

As she rubs her hands over the pocket area she feels something. Curious, she delves inside and brings out a letter, official-looking, could be from a bank, could be from the doctor's. PAM *opens the envelope and her face falls – really concerned. She hears someone return and puts the letter and coat back where she found it.* EDDIE *enters with a bag.*

EDDIE. One pink bikini. Where is she?

> PAM *doesn't answer.*

> Okay… I'm sorry, I overreacted.

> PAM *remains silent.*

> I've said I'm sorry.

> *Silence left hanging.*

> Well? Am I forgiven?

PAM. Why didn't you pay for the picture at the auction?

> *Pause.*

EDDIE (*thrown, but covers*). I've already told you.

PAM. Arh yes, you're going to settle up on Monday.

EDDIE. Does it matter when?

PAM. You tell me?

> *Question left hanging.*

> It was extremely embarrassing. I organised the damn thing and my own husband didn't even pay up.

EDDIE. I'll call them tomorrow if you're that worried.

PAM. I thought we had an early flight.

EDDIE. Well, when we get back. They know I'm good for it.

> (*Calling upstairs.*) Ruby?!

PAM. Leave her.

EDDIE. I want her to come down.

PAM. And what Eddie Carver wants, Eddie Carver gets.

EDDIE. Can we just get back to normal?

PAM. 'Normal'? Okay. You carry on lying and I'll pretend everything's fine.

EDDIE. I don't want any trouble.

PAM. It's not me who ripped the intercom off the wall.

EDDIE (*calling upstairs*). Ruby!

PAM. What's the story, Eddie?

EDDIE (*shouting upstairs*). I want you down here now.

PAM. I know you're hiding something…

EDDIE. I explained why I went to the doctor's. The girl in reception…

PAM. It's not Goldy's staycation I'm worried about.

EDDIE. No rows, not tonight.

PAM. Wouldn't want to spoil our 'quality' time.

> EDDIE *makes to go upstairs.*

> She's not up there.

EDDIE. You said she was upstairs.

PAM. I never.

EDDIE (*panicked*). You let me believe… where is she?

PAM. Not nice, is it? Being kept in the dark.

EDDIE. Pamela?

> PAM *remains silent.*

> Where the hell is she?

PAM. She's gone to see the ponies.

EDDIE. In the stables?

PAM. Unless they've relocated.

EDDIE. I told you both to stay inside.

PAM. I'm not a bloody child.

EDDIE. If she's…

> EDDIE *stops himself saying too much.*

PAM. If she's what? Patted Jasper too vigorously on the nose, gave him one too many carrots…

> *An unearthly scream is heard from the stables* – RUBY.

EDDIE *is frozen to the spot.*

(*Panicked.*) Ruby.

EDDIE. Shit.

PAM. Oh God… Eddie! What the hell…? Well, do something. Eddie!

EDDIE. She's…

PAM. She's what?

EDDIE. She's found it.

PAM. Found what? (*Screaming at him as she runs to the door.*) Found what?

EDDIE. The dog.

Blackout.

End of Act One.

ACT TWO

Scene One

PAM *descends the stairs as* EDDIE *enters with a heavily bloodstained horse rug* (*wrapped around the dead dog*). *He lies it down next to the window.* EDDIE *and* PAM *stare at it.*

PAM. I'm scared, Eddie.

EDDIE. There's no need.

PAM. It's a warning.

EDDIE. That's just [silly]…

PAM. A dead dog…

EDDIE. A horse's head's a warning. Not a dead dog.

PAM. But you are in trouble?

Long pause.

I'm going to ask you this once, Eddie, and I want the truth. Have you started gambling again?

EDDIE. No.

PAM. But someone is chasing you for money? That's why we're holed up in here.

EDDIE. We are not 'holed up' anywhere.

PAM. Is that why we're going away tomorrow?

EDDIE. No.

PAM. Where's the tickets?

EDDIE. What?

PAM. I want to see the tickets.

EDDIE. We pick them up at the airport.

PAM. Are the tickets return?

EDDIE. Course they're bloody return.

PAM. Because Ruby's got exams.

EDDIE. You weren't bothered earlier.

PAM. Well, I am now. (*Beat.*) We're not going.

EDDIE. We've got to.

PAM. Funnily enough, I don't feel like it.

EDDIE. We'll lose the money.

PAM. So?

EDDIE. No point in wasting it.

PAM. You've just spent nine grand on an airbrushed photo of Kerry fucking Katona.

EDDIE. That was for you.

PAM. No, Eddie, it was for you, you locked horns with Trevor and you weren't going to let him beat you. You can't even afford it.

EDDIE. Yes I can.

PAM. I've seen the letter.

EDDIE (*stunned*). What letter?

PAM. You promised me 'never again…' You swore on Ruby's life that you would never gamble.

EDDIE. I haven't set foot inside a casino for years… or a bookies.

PAM. I'm not stupid, Eddie, there's the internet.

EDDIE. I am not gambling.

PAM. Then why is your credit-card company taking you to court?

EDDIE. I've hundreds of credit cards. I've just missed a payment.

PAM. They don't threaten you with court for one missed payment.

EDDIE. How would you know? When did you last pay a bill?

PAM. That's because you won't let me.

EDDIE. I don't want to argue.

PAM. Don't want to argue now, but earlier… you really thought someone was out there.

EDDIE. So did you.

PAM (*processing it all*). No… You even disconnected the phone.

EDDIE. I just wanted us to have a quiet family night.

PAM. It's happening again…

EDDIE. I thought we had an intruder.

PAM. You're expecting somebody. Your gun's usually locked up.

EDDIE. I was cleaning it. I left it out.

PAM. You were going to kill.

EDDIE. I was defending us.

PAM. From who?

EDDIE. Nobody has the right to trespass on my land.

PAM. *Your* land?

EDDIE. You know what I mean.

PAM. You owe people money.

EDDIE. I'm a businessman. Course I owe people money. Everyone owes money.

PAM. Not to the type that go round killing dogs.

EDDIE. They did not kill the dog.

PAM. How do you know? They could be lurking out there now.

EDDIE. They're not.

PAM. Well, someone is.

EDDIE. You didn't say that to Ruby, did you?

PAM. Course not.

EDDIE. I don't want her to be frightened.

PAM. She's devastated.

EDDIE. We've got to make this better.

PAM. And how do you plan to do that? Work a miracle? Raise
    Goldy from the dead? Cos you can't buy your way out of this
    one. We should phone the police.

    PAM *gets her phone from her bag.*

EDDIE. No.

PAM. Why not?

EDDIE. They won't do anything.

PAM. Someone's trespassed.

EDDIE. There's no proof.

PAM. There's a dead dog on my best Persian rug. And unless I'm
    very much mistaken, it didn't commit bloody suicide.

PAM. I want to know who did this.

EDDIE. No you don't.

PAM. I've a right to know.

    EDDIE *takes the phone from her.*

EDDIE. I did.

PAM. What?

EDDIE. It was me.

    Pause. PAM *takes this in.*

EDDIE. I killed the dog.

PAM. *You?* You killed Goldy?

EDDIE. Me.

PAM. You can't have.

EDDIE. I did.

PAM. You're… making this up.

EDDIE. Why would I do that?

PAM. You lie all the time.

EDDIE. I do not.

PAM. You said you didn't know where Goldy was. That was a lie.

EDDIE. Well, I'm not lying now.

PAM. I wish to God you were.

EDDIE. I'm sorry.

PAM. I don't believe this.

EDDIE. You wanted the truth.

PAM. How can I believe anything you say?

EDDIE. I lied to protect Ruby.

PAM. She's heartbroken.

EDDIE. I didn't do it on purpose.

PAM. I should bloody well hope not.

EDDIE. I don't go round killing dogs willy-nilly.

PAM. What happened?

Pause.

EDDIE. I shot it.

PAM. You shot Goldy?

EDDIE. Keep your voice down.

PAM. Why did you…?

EDDIE (*cuts in*). It was in pain.

PAM. What do you mean, 'in pain'? He was fine when we left.

EDDIE. I ran him over.

PAM. You ran him over?

EDDIE. With the horsebox.

PAM. The horsebox? What the hell were you doing in the horsebox?

EDDIE. Moving it… this morning…

PAM. You've kept this from me all day?

EDDIE. I couldn't tell you.

PAM. I'm your wife, Eddie.

EDDIE. Not in front of Ruby.

PAM. I don't believe this.

EDDIE. I didn't want him to suffer. Cruel to be kind.

PAM. Remind me never to get ill.

EDDIE. How is she?

PAM. How do you think she is? She's just seen her pet dog with its brains blown out.

EDDIE. This wasn't meant to happen.

PAM. What do you mean?

EDDIE. What do you mean, what do I mean?

PAM. What you said, what was meant to happen? It sounds like you had a plan.

EDDIE. You're losing it.

PAM. I'm not the one who murdered a dog.

EDDIE. It wasn't murder.

PAM. Tell that to the RSPCA.

EDDIE. I put it out of its misery. They'd probably give me a medal.

PAM. I don't think Ruby's going to see it like that.

RUBY *enters, blowing her nose. She's obviously been crying.*

RUBY. See it like what, Mummy?

PAM. Nothing, darling.

RUBY. It was horrible...

EDDIE. I know.

EDDIE *opens his arms and* RUBY *goes to him.* PAM *can't quite believe how calm and collected* EDDIE*'s being.*

I'm sorry, precious.

RUBY. Did you bring him in?

EDDIE. He's in his favourite spot.

> RUBY *sees Goldy, wrapped in the blanket.*

RUBY. Who'd have done something like this?

PAM. It's probably best you don't know the details.

RUBY. I'm not a child.

EDDIE. Yes you are.

RUBY. I want to know.

> RUBY *goes over to where Goldy is, she strokes the blanket.*
> PAM *and* EDDIE *are really uncomfortable.*

(*To Goldy.*) There, it's warmer in here. I'll look after you now.

PAM. Ruby, darling, I don't think you should be touching him.

RUBY. He's still my dog. (*Beat. To Goldy.*) Who did this to you? What type of monster…

PAM. Darling, don't…

RUBY (*to Goldy*). I'm going to miss you so much.

PAM (*tentatively*). When we get back from our holiday, we could get you a new puppy.

RUBY. Are you being serious?

PAM. Anything to make you happy.

EDDIE. I think it's a great idea, whatever you want.

PAM. She loves those Labradoodles.

RUBY. I want Goldy! I don't *want* a stupid Labradoodle and I don't *want* to go on holiday…

EDDIE. We need something to look forward to.

RUBY. We can't go now.

EDDIE. I know this is hard for you, Ruby, but…

RUBY. Why did you lie?

PAM. Ruby, just…

RUBY. Don't stick up for him.

PAM. I'm not…

RUBY. Why did you say Goldy was at the kennels?

EDDIE *looks to* PAM.

PAM. Your father can explain everything, can't you, Eddie?

EDDIE. Yeah.

PAM. Now I'm going to go and pack. Because we are going away, whether you like it or not. We're your parents and you might not think it now… but we know best.

EDDIE. Your mum's right.

PAM *exits*.

RUBY. Well? Why did you lie?

EDDIE. We should bury him first.

RUBY. And then you'll tell me?

EDDIE. Everything you need to know.

EDDIE *picks up the dog and walks out, followed by* RUBY.

Over this, a whispered voice-over of Ruby reciting verses of Robert Burns's 'To a Mouse', as a video plays of Goldy and Ruby, happy times, having fun.

RUBY. **Wee, sleekit, cowrin, tim'rous beastie,**
    O, what a panic's in thy breastie!
    Thou need na start awa sae hasty
    Wi' bickering brattle!
    I wad be laith to rin an' chase thee,
    Wi' murdering pattle!

   Thou saw the fields laid bare an' waste,
    An' weary winter comin fast,
    An' cozie here, beneath the blast,
    Thou thought to dwell,
    Till crash! the cruel coulter past
    Out thro' thy cell.

   But Mousie, thou art no thy lane,
    In proving foresight may be vain:

The best laid schemes o' Mice an' Men
Gang aft agley,
An' lea'e us nought but grief an' pain,
For promis'd joy!

Still, thou are blest, compared wi' me!
The present only toucheth thee:
But Och! I backward cast my e'e,
On prospects drear!
An' forward, tho' I canna see,
I guess an' fear!

Scene Two

EDDIE *and* RUBY *enter, having just buried Goldy.*

RUBY. You should have called the vet.

EDDIE. He would have put him down. Better to get it over with quickly.

RUBY. Are you sure he couldn't have survived?

EDDIE. I didn't have a choice. It was over in a flash, he didn't feel a thing.

RUBY. How can you know?

EDDIE. Trust me, Rube.

RUBY. You can't know for certain.

EDDIE. He didn't suffer.

RUBY. He must have been in pain from the accident… he was by himself, all alone… I should have been with him.

EDDIE. I was there.

RUBY. But you must have gone inside to get the gun?

EDDIE (*wrong-footed*). I was quick.

RUBY. Was he scared?

EDDIE. He didn't even know it was happening.

RUBY. Did he look up at you when you put the gun to his head?

EDDIE. Ruby.

RUBY. Goldy's a gun dog, he knows what damage a gun can do.

EDDIE. He didn't have a clue.

RUBY. Did you look into his eyes?

EDDIE *doesn't answer.*

Did you?

Pause.

EDDIE. Yes.

RUBY. What did you see?

Silence.

I want to know.

EDDIE. Trust.

RUBY (*relieved*). Just like horses.

EDDIE *waits for further explanation, but* RUBY *is in a world of her own.* EDDIE *is uncomfortable but tries to hide it.*

Such sensitive creatures for their size. Intelligent animals. So you think they'd know when they were about to be killed. But they don't. It's quite a skill, shooting a horse. There's a technique they use, to minimise suffering. Draw an imaginary cross from the horse's left ear to right eye and then the same on the other side, hold the gun perpendicular and fire. You've got to get the angle right, the shot needs to travel down the spine to kill it instantly. I've seen it done.

India's dad's a vet. He was giving us a lift home from school when he got the call. There'd been an accident. Some horses had been running loose on a country road and one of them had been hit by a car. It was in a bad way. Broken leg. They managed to keep hold of it, nostrils flaring, fear in its eyes. We were told to stay in the car, not to watch, but we couldn't help it, we were transfixed. This magnificent creature... I'd never seen a horse like it – dark liver chestnut, in its prime. The owner had to hold it. Keep it calm while India's dad lined up the gun. Those beautiful brown eyes. Then… (*Pause.*) They use a silencer… so not a big bang, but there is a finality to the sound. And after… the thud. There was a small hole in its forehead, like a little star, but inside… so much damage. The horse was lying on the ground twitching and the girl started wailing, an unbearable sound… grief and guilt. She was the one who'd let them out. They couldn't afford to keep them. And they couldn't afford to put them down properly. The girl knew that the hunt would be round to collect them. She couldn't bear to think of her beloved horses being eaten by a pack of hounds. So she tried to set them free.

EDDIE. You never said anything.

RUBY. You were never around to tell.

EDDIE. You shouldn't have had to see that.

RUBY. You can't protect me from everything, Daddy.

EDDIE. I can try.

Beat.

RUBY. Poor Goldy.

EDDIE. I'm sorry.

RUBY. For what it's worth, I think you're brave. I couldn't have pulled the trigger. Are you all right?

EDDIE. It's been a tough day.

RUBY. You should have told us earlier.

EDDIE. I… couldn't.

RUBY. We're stronger than you think.

RUBY *kisses him and walks away.*

EDDIE. Ruby? What happened to the girl…?

RUBY. I don't know… but when we drove past today, the house was up for sale.

RUBY *goes upstairs.* EDDIE *buries his head in his hands.*

Lights fade as –

CCTV flickers on and a recent family video plays (improvised by actors) happy times – Eddie, testing out his new top-of-the-range camcorder.

PAM *enters and watches* EDDIE.

PAM. Eddie, we need to…

EDDIE (*exiting*). Not now…

RUBY *appears at the top of the stairs in her pyjamas.*

RUBY. Mum.

PAM (*painting on a smile*). What, darling?

RUBY. I don't feel very well.

PAM. Come here.

They meet on the stairs and PAM *gives her a hug.*

RUBY. I'm sorry.

PAM. What have you got to be sorry about?

RUBY. For being a brat.

PAM. You're bound to be upset.

RUBY. It just feels wrong, going away when we've just buried Goldy.

PAM. I know, but he wouldn't want you to be upset, now, would he?

RUBY. No.

PAM. And after the night we've had, we could do with a holiday.

RUBY (*unconvinced*). I suppose so.

PAM. If you really don't want to go… we'll cancel it.

RUBY. Really?

PAM. Really.

RUBY. You'd cancel your dream holiday for me?

PAM. If that's what you want… anything to make you happy…

RUBY. Anything?

PAM. Anything.

RUBY. Would you go bra-less and wear tie-dye?

PAM. Don't push it, Rubes.

They laugh, enjoying the moment.

RUBY. You're right, we should go, but I haven't packed or anything.

PAM. It's all right, we'll get up really early and do it then.

RUBY. I don't know what to take.

PAM. It doesn't matter what you take, you'd look beautiful in an old sack. (*Lightly.*) I hate you.

RUBY (*playing along*). Not as much as I hate you.

PAM. Bet I do.

RUBY. Don't.

PAM. Do.

RUBY. Don't.

PAM. Don't.

RUBY. Do.

PAM. Got you.

Both laughing.

RUBY. Arr… I can't believe I fell for that.

PAM. Twice in one night!

RUBY. Thanks, Mum.

PAM. What for?

RUBY. For being you.

PAM. I thought you preferred India's mum?

RUBY. She's not as funny as you.

PAM. Well, that's no good.

RUBY. She's never once made me laugh.

PAM. Maybe she left her sense of humour on a kibbutz in Timbuktu?

RUBY. Probably. (*Beat.*) I've been thinking… I'm not going to go travelling.

PAM. Ruby, you don't have to say that for me…

RUBY. I don't want to, not now.

PAM. Well, we don't have to make a decision tonight, why don't you get some sleep and we'll see how we feel in the morning.

RUBY. Yeah, thanks, Mum.

RUBY *kisses* PAM *goodnight.*

PAM. You do know that me and Daddy love you very much.

RUBY *nods.* EDDIE *enters with a tray, a mug of cocoa with marshmallows for* RUBY, *an open bottle of champagne in a bucket for* PAM, *and a bottle of beer for himself.*

EDDIE (*upbeat*). Is someone taking my name in vain?

PAM. We're talking about you, not to you.

EDDIE *hands* RUBY *her cocoa.*

EDDIE. Your favourite.

RUBY. Marshmallows, you're spoiling me.

EDDIE. I'm your dad, that's my job.

She gives him a peck on the cheek.

RUBY. Night.

EDDIE. Goodnight, sweetheart.

He goes to give her a big hug but the cocoa is in the way.

PAM. Give it here.

PAM *takes the cocoa. As they hug…*

RUBY. I love you, Daddy.

EDDIE. I love you. I'm so sorry…

RUBY. Don't mention Goldy, I'll start crying again.

PAM. C'mon, you, up the wooden hill to Bedfordshire.

She hands RUBY *her cocoa, who goes upstairs to bed.* PAM *waits until* RUBY *is out of sight.* EDDIE *starts pouring* PAM *a drink. During the scene,* EDDIE *will make sure* PAM *drinks the champagne.* PAM *will gradually become tired, drowsy.*

PAM *starts clapping slowly.*

What a performance. The concerned father.

EDDIE. We've just buried her dog.

PAM. And whose fault's that? (*Beat, then re: the drinks.*) What's all this, a wake for Goldy? Because, I don't know about you, but I'm sick of champagne.

EDDIE. Come on, Pam.

PAM. Just because you've pulled the wool over her eyes, don't think I'm fooled.

EDDIE. Relax. Have a drink.

PAM. I'd rather have a clear head.

EDDIE. It's your favourite.

She necks a glass in one, to prove a point.

PAM. Satisfied? Now, what the hell is going on?

EDDIE. Nothing…

PAM. I watched the CCTV.

EDDIE. You did what?

PAM. While you two were having your little heart-to-heart.

EDDIE. You can't even work it.

PAM. I'm nobody's fool, Eddie.

EDDIE. I can't believe you tried to check up on me.

PAM. What's good for the goose…

EDDIE. I don't snoop on you.

PAM. No, you pay somebody else to do it.

EDDIE. It's called delegation.

PAM. It's called paranoia. He was my personal trainer! Before
     you scared him off.

EDDIE. I didn't trust him, his shorts were too tight.

PAM. 'Trust'! You're a fine one to speak.

EDDIE. Oh, I was wondering when you'd throw this back in my
     face.

PAM. The affairs I could handle. It's the lies I can't stand. (*Pause*.)
     Surely Eddie Carver's not lost for words? The big man, silver-
     tongued charmer who can talk his way out of anything?

EDDIE. Don't be like…

PAM (*cuts in*). Since you told me about Goldy, something's been
     nagging away…

EDDIE. Yeah… you.

PAM. The horsebox hadn't moved. It was in exactly the same
     place as this morning. And if the horsebox hadn't moved, the
     dog couldn't have been run over.

EDDIE. I moved it and then I parked it back in the same place.

PAM. Arrh… that explains it.

EDDIE. See, problem solved. You've been watching too much
     Midsomer Murders.

PAM. That's probably it. Mind, it doesn't explain how you drove
     it when I had the keys.

EDDIE. What?

PAM. The keys were in my bag.

EDDIE. I used the spare set.

PAM. There isn't a spare set.

EDDIE. I had some cut.

PAM. Where are they?

EDDIE. You don't believe me?

PAM. I don't know what to believe.

EDDIE. Have another drink.

PAM. That's your answer to everything.

EDDIE. You've never complained before.

PAM. Where are the keys, Eddie?

EDDIE. I don't know, they'll be around somewhere. Er, forgive me if I'm not on top form, but it's been quite a day. This whole business with Goldy...

PAM. Poor Eddie.

EDDIE. I was really upset.

PAM. You didn't look upset – on the CCTV.

Growing concern from EDDIE.

Wonderful system. Very clear pictures. Worth every penny.

EDDIE. You're...

PAM. Lying? Not me. Ruby's been teaching her stupid old mummy how to use the security system.

EDDIE. What did you see?

PAM. What do you think? (*Pause.*) You and Goldy looked like you were having a great time. You, Goldy and the shotgun.

PAM *uses the remote to play the CCTV footage through the TV –*

Eddie with the gun, playing with the healthy dog. He holds the gun to Goldy's head as if to shoot... it's all a big game.

PAM *rewinds it, plays it again...*

EDDIE. It isn't what it looks like.

PAM. There was no accident, was there?

EDDIE *is lost for words.*

Least not with the horsebox.

EDDIE. I lied… about the horsebox.

PAM. What else are you lying about?

Pause.

EDDIE. Nothing. Look, I'd taken him for a walk, up in the woods, I wanted to do some target practice.

PAM. 'Target practice'?

EDDIE. There's a competition at the club next week, I needed to practice on live targets…

A look of horror fills PAM*'s face.*

PAM. Oh my God!

EDDIE. No… not the dog, the dog was a mistake.

PAM. You mean an accident?

EDDIE. Accident… mistake… same difference. We were walking through the woods… I tripped and fell… and the gun went off. Simple.

PAM. Why didn't you just say?

EDDIE. I didn't want Ruby to find out.

PAM. Well, she was going to find out sooner or later. You can't disguise a headless dog for long.

EDDIE. Such a mess.

PAM. If it happened in the woods, why didn't you just leave him there?

EDDIE. I don't know… I wasn't really thinking straight. Foxes. The foxes would have got him.

PAM. Why didn't you just tell me? Why make up all this stuff? You had me thinking all sorts…

EDDIE. Like what?

PAM. I don't know, like maybe you were having some sort of breakdown.

EDDIE. A 'breakdown'?

PAM. It happens.

EDDIE. Not to me it doesn't.

PAM. We all feel under pressure from time to time, depression's rife at the moment.

EDDIE. Let's get one thing straight. I am not depressed. I don't do depression. I haven't got time to be depressed. Anyway, I'm not the type.

PAM. There isn't a 'type'…

EDDIE. Depression is an excuse for the miserable and work-shy. Bloody whiners the lot of them.

PAM. So Trevor's a whiner?

EDDIE. Trevor? What's he got to do with it?

PAM. He's on antidepressants.

EDDIE. Bollocks!

PAM. I'm telling you.

EDDIE. There's no way…

PAM. Viv told me.

EDDIE (*genuinely shocked*). What the hell's Viv telling you something like that for?

PAM. She's my best friend.

EDDIE. Oh, and I suppose all this will be reported back to Viv, will it?

PAM. Course not.

EDDIE. I'm sure Trevor doesn't want his business being discussed by half the bloody county.

PAM. I am not 'half the bloody county'.

EDDIE. She shouldn't have told you.

PAM. It's not my fault.

EDDIE. You'll have encouraged her.

PAM. I did not.

EDDIE. I know what you're like when you get together. Gossiping. Our business is our business.

PAM. I wouldn't talk about... you.

Snort of derision from EDDIE.

EDDIE. And I am not having a bloody breakdown.

PAM. Then why were you at the doctor's?

Pause as she waits for his answer, with growing frustration.

Well, it wasn't to arrange a sleepover for Goldy, because he was already in doggy heaven. What's going on, Eddie?

EDDIE *remains silent*.

We can get through this, whatever it is. You've just got to tell me the truth.

EDDIE. The truth...

PAM. I'll make it easy, should I? Well, you're either screwing that bimbo receptionist or you've got the clap. And I don't know which I prefer.

A weak laugh from EDDIE *as he shakes his head*.

EDDIE. She's not much older than Ruby.

PAM. Never stopped you before.

EDDIE. Well, that was then.

PAM. We haven't had sex for months.

EDDIE. What about this morning?

PAM (*dismissing*). Apart from that...

EDDIE. Never usually bothers you.

PAM. Well, it does if I think you're getting it elsewhere. I am not letting some little trollop ruin over twenty-five years of...

EDDIE (*cuts in*). Fighting talk.

PAM. Too bloody right. I've invested everything into this marriage and nobody is going to take what's mine.

EDDIE. Are you talking about me or my money?

PAM. You're a package, Eddie. One doesn't exist without the other.

EDDIE. You could walk away.

PAM. And do what, exactly? Because there's not much call for over-the-hill ex-beauty queens.

EDDIE. You could go back to your mother.

PAM. Are you being serious? I'm not going anywhere with my tail between my legs. (*Pause*.) You're going to leave, aren't you?

EDDIE. Maybe it'd be for the best.

PAM. You're scaring me, Eddie.

EDDIE. Please, don't be [scared]…

PAM. I can't believe you'd throw it all away…

EDDIE. I'm not.

PAM. When I made those wedding vows, *I* meant them.

EDDIE. Do you really think we can survive anything?

PAM. What choice do we have?

Pause.

EDDIE. I'm… not having an affair.

PAM. You're not?

EDDIE. No, and I haven't got the clap or any other sexually transmitted disease.

PAM. I don't understand. Then why…? (*Beat, the penny drops*.) Oh my God. (*Pause, fixed on him*.) No…

EDDIE. Don't worry.

PAM. I'm a born worrier.

EDDIE. Well, stop it.

PAM. It's cancer, isn't it?

EDDIE. No.

PAM. You've got cancer.

EDDIE. It's not... it's just... embarrassing.

PAM. Testicular cancer?

EDDIE. No.

PAM. Prostate?

EDDIE. What?

PAM. Prostate cancer. Up your bum. That's why you didn't want to tell me.

EDDIE. I have not got arse cancer or bollock cancer or any other bloody type of cancer.

PAM. So you're not dying?

EDDIE. Don't sound so disappointed.

PAM. Are you dying or not?

EDDIE. We're all dying, just some will go quicker than others.

PAM. You're not helping.

EDDIE. I do not have a terminal illness.

> PAM *is on the verge of tears, possibly relief.*

Don't get upset, please.

PAM. I'm sorry. It's just... I can't help thinking the worst... sometimes I lie awake at night worrying about how it could all go wrong... but that's a good thing because you only ever think like that when you've got something worth losing. If anything happened to you... if you died... if you left me...

EDDIE. I'm not going to leave you. I love you, Pam, now more than ever.

PAM. And you're definitely not going to die on me?

EDDIE. I promise.

PAM. Then why did you go to the doctor's?

> *Pause.*

EDDIE. I needed some sleeping tablets.

PAM. You?

EDDIE. I've had trouble sleeping.

PAM. You never said.

EDDIE. I didn't want to worry you.

PAM. Everyone needs a little help from time to time.

EDDIE. Yeah well, not usually me.

PAM. You're human, Eddie, we've all got our weaknesses.

EDDIE. You don't seem to have any.

PAM. You're mine. Always have been. You're doing the right thing…

EDDIE. Am I?

PAM. Taking time off, spending it with us. That's how it should be. We're a family. We'll always be here for you…

EDDIE. Always?

PAM. You're not getting rid of me that easily. Till death us do part.

EDDIE. Tired?

PAM. All this talk is making me sleepy.

    EDDIE *smiles*, RUBY *appears at the top of the stairs, very sleepy.*

RUBY. Dad…

PAM. You should be in bed, we've got an early start.

RUBY. I need a cuddle.

EDDIE. It's fine… give her five minutes. Come on, sleepyhead.

    RUBY *joins them on the sofa. And snuggles up to* EDDIE.

RUBY. Daddy, do pets go to heaven?

EDDIE. Course they do, darling.

RUBY. India doesn't believe in heaven.

PAM. What does she know?

EDDIE. Goldy's probably up there now, annoying everybody with his squeaky bone.

RUBY (*content*). Yeah.

RUBY *slips into unconsciousness.*

PAM. She's shattered, bless her.

EDDIE. It's been a long day.

PAM. We still haven't finished the Monopoly.

EDDIE. We'll take it with us.

PAM. On holiday?

EDDIE. I might even let you win.

PAM. Promises… promises…

EDDIE. I would.

PAM. I didn't fall in love with a loser.

EDDIE. I love you, Mrs Carver.

PAM *smiles as she slips into unconsciousness.*

Lights fade.

Voices over…

MAN. He seemed like a nice bloke, a real family man.

WOMAN. We're all devastated.

GIRL. She had her whole life ahead of her.

WOMAN. You don't expect something like this to happen, not on your own doorstep.

Scene Three

EDDIE. There, this is nice, isn't it? A nice family night, no more silly disturbances. (*Catches sight of the picture of Kerry Katona.*) You, young lady, nearly got me caught out. Even the best-laid plans can go wrong, ask Rabbie Burns's mouse... or Gerald Ratner – five hundred million for a prawn sandwich, ouch! Still, we're here now. Right where we should be. Together.

EDDIE *starts brushing* RUBY*'s hair.*

You know, Pamela, I don't think I've brushed Ruby's hair since she was a baby. 'You never did then, too busy empire-building.' Damned if you do, damned if you don't, eh, Rubes? How do you want it? Best leave it down, more comfortable for a nice long sleep. When you were a little girl, I used to tiptoe into your bedroom and watch you in the land of nod... so peaceful, not a worry in the world. (*Pause, then a little laugh as he remembers*.) I remember once you woke from a nightmare, screaming... crying so hard you couldn't catch your breath... clinging to me, telling Daddy about the scary big buzzy-bee that was chasing you. The most terrifying thing in your world was a big buzzy-bee. Oh, to be a child again... You are so beautiful. Just like your mother. My beauty queen and my princess.

(*To* PAM.) I'm sorry I had to keep things from you, but honesty isn't always the best policy. We all lie... sometimes big whoppers, other times little white lies. It oils the wheels of life. (*Re: Kerry.*) Look at her lot, presenting an image to the world, and inside they could be dying. We're all living a lie... it's just a question of scale... (*Little laugh.*) Apparently, you're right, men do have an ability to compartmentalise, to shut off. Experiences... emotions... we just flick a switch, turn a key, lock them away in the safe deposit box and carry on. You make out it's a bad thing. But I was ambling along just fine, until the letter came. Not the one you found, no, there's hundreds like that. *The* letter.

EDDIE *picks up his phone and starts to dial.*

We're going to show them, Pam, nobody fucks with Eddie Carver. Nobody. (*On phone.*) Gerry! How's my favourite bank manager? You really should answer your phone, you shouldn't advertise a twenty-four-hour banking service if you're not going to deliver. People hate speaking to machines, but I'm not complaining, not tonight. You'll probably pick this up Monday morning, lovely start to the working week. Did you have a nice weekend with the wife and kids? Me too... the best ever.

EDDIE *sings the chorus of Joni Mitchell's 'Big Yellow Taxi'. Then puts the phone on speakerphone, putting it down.*

Can you still hear me, Gerry? How much do you love your family? Because I love mine to death. And it's my job to provide for them. To protect them. Keep them safe, keep them happy. But you helped screw that up, didn't you? Happy to bankroll when you're flush – 'Yes, Mr Carver, no, Mr Carver, three bags fucking full, Mr Carver.' But when times are tough... when you're starting to struggle... Like rats deserting a sinking ship. Leaving me to drown. Every rat for himself.

EDDIE *brings out the gun and starts to clean it.*

Have you ever killed anything, Gerry? No, thought not. Wouldn't want to get your hands dirty. Well, not properly. You haven't got the balls. I have. It's a messy business. Not like shooting grouse. Anyone can kill from a distance. You don't have to look into their eyes. I'm a fully fledged member of an exclusive club. No room for cowards. Goldy's a very trusting dog. So when I put the barrel of the gun to his head, he actually licked it, as though it was some sort of game. Seeing those little dark eyes looking up at me... my finger poised on the trigger... I needed to test myself. See if I'd be able to... it was easier than I thought. I talked to him in that little doggy voice he loves. He was so excited, jumping up, wagging his tail. He didn't suspect a thing. One squeeze and he was dead. Better to go quick than to suffer. (*Beat.*) This gun is handmade. Beautiful workmanship. Seventy grand's worth.

EDDIE *picks up the remote and points it at the TV.*

Chris de Burgh's 'Lady in Red' plays...

Our favourite, Pam. Our first wedding dance. Would you like to...? I don't want to embarrass Ruby and I know she thinks this is naff... You don't mind, do you, precious?

EDDIE *starts to dance with an unconscious* PAM. *He sings and occasionally talks to her.*

You do trust me, don't you? It's all for the best.

Can you remember when I first brought you here? You thought we were just coming for a nosey around. I'd arranged with the estate agent to keep the 'For Sale' sign up. When we drove up the gravel drive, your face was a picture. This place *was* the wow factor... I could see Ruby in the rear-view mirror... wide-eyed, fixed on the stables and the paddock... And you couldn't bear it. 'Stop, Eddie, because if I see it, I'll want it and this place is gonna cost the earth.' But I didn't stop, I kept driving, because this was our dream home and we so deserved it.

You didn't have to worry, I haven't been gambling. Well, not in the sense you meant. (*Quoting his own words with irony.*) 'Business is about taking risks. If you're not prepared to put your neck on the line you shouldn't be in the game.' This time I'm going down and it's legit. I've played the game but the casinos seem to have changed the rules. They're refusing to give me any more chips. Bankers, eh...? Cheating, money-grabbing bastards, the lot. I've worked hard for all this and nobody is going to take it from me. The bailiffs are coming. But I'm going to make a stand. This is my castle and I'm pulling up the drawbridge. If I can't have it, then nobody else will.

EDDIE *takes a Zippo lighter out of his pocket, flicks it open, flicks it closed.*

Pamela, we're going out in style.

EDDIE *lies* PAM *down next to* RUBY *as if she is cradling her daughter.* EDDIE *picks up the gun and points it.*

'Lady in Red' comes to an end. Chris de Burgh whispers 'I love you' as the lights fade.

Voices over…

MAN. We just can't understand it.

WOMAN. What a waste.

Gunshot.

WOMAN. He doted on them.

GIRL. They seemed like the perfect family.

Gunshot.

EDDIE *reloads the gun, sits down next to* PAM *and* RUBY, *and places the barrel under his chin.*

MAN. They had everything… Just goes to show…

CCTV flickers on –

Eddie and Pam exit the church to cheers and confetti…

BEST MAN. Go on, Eddie, give her a kiss…

EDDIE. Come here, gorgeous…

Eddie kisses her.

BEST MAN. Now look at the camera… Say something… Make it special, you'll be able to show this to the grandkids.

PAM. Isn't my husband – (*Squeals with delight.*) the best…

EDDIE. I love you, Mrs Carver…

PAM. I'm the luckiest woman in the whole world.

Gunshot. Screens freeze.

Flames engulf the wedding picture onscreen as we hear a fire raging through the manor.

Blackout.

The End.

My thanks to...

Chris Monks for his unflinching quiet bravery, in allowing me to write a play about a very difficult subject and having faith in me to deliver.

Noreen Kershaw for her ever-positive attitude; for embracing this new play, having her own ambitious vision for it and being such a bloody good laugh.

Andrew Dunn, Julie Riley and Jodie Comer who have taken the characters and added another layer, making the Carvers better than I ever imagined. It's been a delight to work with you all.

Stephen Wood and all the wonderful staff at the Stephen Joseph Theatre who make it such a very special place to work. I won't name you all because there isn't room and I'd hate to miss anyone out, but my sincere thanks to each and every one of you.

Martin Belderson, Denise Gilfoyle, the SJT OutReach Community Actors and all those who contributed to the making of the video. We couldn't have done it without your generosity.

Tim Meacock & Jim Simmons (Lighting) for their beautiful designs and for keeping their parachutes open.

Maggie Tully (our lovely DSM) for being such an organised and positive presence in the rehearsal room.

For help with research and initial script development...

David Grouse, Liz Lorrimar, Jim & Sue Turner.

Christine Chapman, Joy Gatenby & the girls at Church High School, Newcastle.

Deborah Bruce, Steve Cooper, Tess Denman-Cleaver.

Tally Garner for her invaluable advice and support. Nick Marston, Sarah Chadwick and all at Curtis Brown.

Nick Hern and all the staff at NHB, especially Jodi Gray for her patience and eagle-eyed proofing.

Janine Birkett, for providing the best bed and breakfast in Scarborough.

My fabulous and ever-supportive family and friends.

Fiona Evans, 2010